Crossings

Franchot Ballinger

Fernwood
PRESS

Crossings

Fernwood Press
Newberg, Oregon
www.fernwoodpress.com

Printed in the United States of America

Cover and page design: Mareesa Fawver Moss
Cover photo: Julie Blake Edison via Unsplash
Author photo: Rich James

ISBN 978-1-59498-089-3

Franchot very much wanted to see this book in print.
Unfortunately, he passed away before his dream was realized.

We have been honored to help shepherd
this book through the final stages before publication.
We so wish he could have seen this project to completion.

Franchot L. Ballinger
1939–2021

Respectfully,
Henrietta, Robert, Julie, and Elise Ballinger

For Henrietta

"The love of one woman"
—W.S. Merwin

How can there be such singularity?
All around us are multiplications,
exponential effusions of professions,
of declaration, of protestation, of procreation.
All the lavish universe refuses a center,
denies a focus—galaxy, nebula, black hole,
all teeming and sucking and wildly flung,
all's akimbo, flailing, flying,
even the million seeds of the white pine
like stars carried promiscuously afar.

But look—she who is a wealth of caresses,
wellspring of kisses, creates with me a center,
a holdfast root to flower, as if
we were the only and last of our kind:
precious and prayerful, all stem and stalk,
leaf and flavor, bloom and blossom,
seed and husk, juice of fruit and pulp.
Sunk in guttering light and
darkening sweep of cosmos,
of our days, our lives, there is only
this one love—avant-garde acceptance,
cool conspicuousness (if puzzling principle),
remarkable reaping.

Table of Contents

I

Now softly the flutes
of deepest night sigh, broken reeds of grief.

Adam, Where Are You?

I wasn't long for that world.
I was treated like dirt.
OK, so I didn't get to choose my
name, but I'm my own man, I'll tell you.
I got to name the filthy beasts,
who were already there when I
woke from that dreamless, selfless sleep
I'd been in. What a greeting they gave me—
their snarling bared teeth, claws, and hooves
mauling the air before me.
They were something else, and I
was more than glad to say what they were.
It was like the names kept them off.

Then *she* happened, sudden.
I woke from a nap (this one a dreaming-of-me
sleep). And there she was. Now, where'd she come from?
Not something I could (or would have) dreamt up.
I got to name her, too: Eve.
Prophetic, eh?
If such things as beasts and she must be,
there's comfort in giving a name.
Still, the orders were to take her
as my flesh and bone. One,
we were supposed to be—like lichen or pondlight,
I guess—as if there were no edges to us.

What a puzzle. But, you know,
sometimes that being one stuff wasn't bad.
I'd wake in the morning from my dreams,
her head on my chest,
and the light would be like a lilt in the air—
a choral radiance greeting us—and we
smiled a lot in a certain dim-witted way.

But most often, we'd stand staring at each other,
dull as dirt, stunned as deer caught in torchlight.
She clearly wasn't me, and I wasn't her,
not that I cared to be. So, all in all, I for one
was only too glad to get out. Never mind the rumors—
I chose.
During all the "he said, she said" after the trouble,
I felt something crack inside, like a flawed pot
overheated in all the hiss and boil of the tiff.
From then on, it was all careless looks and words
flicked like snot from fingertips.
The light in her eyes flew off
like a puff of milkweed down across an empty field at dusk.
I saw there was nothing
between us but echoing air. I
couldn't stay, had to be free, and left in dark of night.

But then, there *she* was. I
could sense her skulking out behind me. I
didn't look for fear I'd get yanked back. Maybe
I should have; maybe the old evil eye
would have sent her back. But she
caught up, and we stumbled along.

As we still do.

Now, most days and in the long, long
nights, we scarcely converse.
When we do, our voices seem to caress themselves,
and something in them spills and spills
like rain down denuded hills.

Keeping the Distance

"There is a distance where magnets pull"
—Kay Ryan

Attraction haunts us like hounds.
Along trails lie lodestones
of yearning, lure

of inclination, inducement's allure
to coupling harmony, sweetmeat
enticement's pull. All

magnetism subverts balance,
mars distance until one fails
to falling. Well may we claw

and scratch against gravity:
when longing draws, is drawn
over, circumference collapses,
center crashes.

Earth rightly rides this galaxy rim: all
that stays afloat must swing for periphery.

The Judas Tree

The redbud tree in my backyard
is cousin to the Judas tree
from which Iscariot hanged himself
in an agony of guilt.
"I have betrayed an innocent,"
he grieved. "What's that to us," they laughed,
and so he hanged himself. The tree
had its own innocence, but shame

turned its white flowers bloody red.
Another's sin disgraced the tree
Cercis siliquastrum.
My tree, the *canadensis*, blooms
6,000 miles away,
so what's that to me?

Cold Spell

The cold calligraphy of winter trees
spells silence—not a quiet time of thought
or reverie but desolation. Wrought
chiaroscuro in this midnight freeze,
the branches close like cruel parentheses
about the empty night air that begot
this cold calligraphy.

The wind has gone with all its minor keys
and left a longing, left a darkened spot.
Now you look out and know your heart cannot
see light but, through the silence, only sees
this cold calligraphy.

Cain Killed Abel

Cain killed Abel in jealous rage;
God branded Cain, then set him free.
Cain's crime was of the first degree,
guilt he hoped leaving could assuage.

Cain wandered, married, set the stage
to modify his history.
Cain killed Abel in jealous rage;
God branded Cain, then set him free.

Cain found he couldn't leave that stage
in mind on which repeatedly
he struck, drew blood, heard God's decree.
Thus Cain begot a heritage.

Cain killed Abel in jealous rage;
God branded Cain, then set us free.

Love and All the Green

It's summer. Love and all the green
pricks us alive (as long as morning's new.
By noon, heat clogs the dusty window screen.)
It's summer, Love; and all the green
in all the world has stammered on like neon
to flood our way with weediness
and summer love, and all the green
pricks us alive—so long as morning's new.

Climate Change

Jeremiah 2:13

The old stories tell us.
High in the mountains,
a meadow, its life-bearing breath snowlocked in winter,
in spring and summer a passionate release
streams of living waters,

a pure tumbling down to the city
the water rolling, an ever-flowing stream.

So the old stories say.

Now the witch's brew of our days—alchemy
of desire and fear—rises, chokes the meadow,
a few pools, a deathly sheen,
a trickle of spittle in a sun-baked trench.

Ask the trees; they will tell you.
Their parched tongues whisper
in the gray winds, and their limbs sign
above the cleft wells of our hearts.

Snow Furies

It's snowing this morning
in a Christmas card sort of way.
From my desk, I watch the flakes
in their fluttering descent,
little angels come to call upon us.
But an old man intrudes
into the alluring snow light,
his windbreaker a dark field
the angels founder into.
He appeared there yesterday
as I returned home,
as if the winter's squalid light
had transfigured itself into him,
a body to ask me for a quarter,
which I gave (having many in my pocket),
gave and wished him—
one of the haunting unhoused—away.
And now he's come again,
looking this way,
a witness,
the Ghost of Charity Past,
while the snow
beats against my windows.

<—>

sufficiency a horizon line
I never reach, only
here; this desire wire
on which I teeter

In the Dark Belly of Assumption

With the certainty of dread, I know
there are snakes here. Rattler. Copperhead.
Worse. Under the ledges, along the root
swarming trail, or in the wilderness
of leaf litter on hillsides, one waits
out of the day's heat, dark mind
in savage solitude.

Walking alone, I can
imagine two lightning darts at my ankle
or my caught breath, a hand misplaced
yanked back, and there's the stigmata
of my heedlessness, the malice already
caught up in the swift current
to my heart.
    But then, what do they know
of me? Does one lie shrouded
in leaf dust and instinct, tense
in dread expectancy of the flash
and rock clack of my hiking staff,
in some twilight nightmare of my
boot heel cracking the delicate
bowl of its skull?

    Two darknesses
each remembering the other, and day
wearing on to nightfall.

Floating in This Dark

after Georg Trakl's "Grodek"

It's nightfall again. The plains lose their golden light,
promises that can't be kept, and the blue lakes
are circumstanced darkly. Oaks cry out in wind voices

like bayonets, their leaves clattering like scabbards against legs.
Tramped paths lead through the grass to fallen bodies. Quietly,

in a meadow corner, as if the gathering red clouds
of God's presence, blood pools, cool as the moon.
The shadows, settling, regard dying boys
from whose slashed mouths leap wild cries.

Beneath the shining thorns of the stars, a sister's or wife's ghost
like a moth flutters down over a corpse, kisses the hero,

caresses his crown of blood. Now softly the flutes
of deepest nights sigh, broken reeds of grief.
On a little hill like an altar, pain feeds spirit's flame,
and all its children float in this dark, thick as fireflies.

Passion Painting with No Goldfinches

The goldfinches have left.
They have gathered up the air
                            beneath their black-robed wings
and shaken off the dust of our dusty world.

Abandoned thistle, crown of thorns;
broken bone stalk;
                            and morning air, cloak
of our salvation, rent in absence.

What's left?
Pentimenti of hopes
                            in a dissolving frame.
Only, try to remember the endless knot of their song.

||

a flowing and a standing still
a step, a lingering, a step

That Moment

This day, what might have been, what is.
There was that moment
(like Orpheus about to look over his shoulder
not seeing yet either behind or ahead).

On the Hope-Thin Highwire

believing
a flowing and a standing still
a step, a lingering, a step
a sort of stillness
balancing
for all one knows
over desolation
feeling the way
teetering
gingerly
sliding forward
still
hanging back—
ahead
a voice from the blinding light?

Countenance

Never invited, they disquiet my days—
their comings, their goings.
(Enter stage left. Exit stage right.)
One watches me (quality control)
as I shave, seeing the scratches, noting
the bent nails, the head a little
off-kilter, some misalignment of the
eyes, the whole fit so loose
there's daylight through the cracks.
Or another the eyes of sorrow-song longing.
Then there's that one I catch sight of
in a storefront window, with his look that says,
"I've seen plenty and could tell if asked."
And odd moments, the solitaire grieving
absence,
not so much as a shadow.
And more. So many.
Some I hardly know.
They're all still around at bedtime
like nesting Russian dolls.
But then waiting
for sleep's dark prayer,
on my deepest horizon,
a shining.

When I Remember Thee upon My Bed

Sleep.
Secret room of unspoken prayer.
The door shut against me,
again.

Released

Ah—this Self.
Sometimes a stinking corpse.
Then the pyre of prayer
and everything up in flame.

When I Remember These Things

As the deer pants for streams of water—
I know the yearning, thirst, grief
of finding the streambed September dry,
and how, as days pass into night, clouds
gather their promises and leave, then
a mute sky and last light an empty pane.
The little winds no longer a breathing
into but like the stinging hiss of sand
that takes my breath away until I am parched
with desire, looking into Abraham's sky,
waiting for what the stars will bring,
a night bird scorning, *Where? Where?*
I remember these things until the longing
feels like rain, and I open my hands,
and the thirst becomes fire.

Let Me Be Like Those Who Dream

"All Christian thinking is resurrection thinking."
—Jay Parini

Let this sorrow be a fallow field
and grief the seeding rain.
Then may I be hidden, a grain
in night's still mystery,
until the day
I'm risen, yield
bound in sheaves of joy,
and Negev is an ecstasy.

This Cup

waits to be filled, perhaps longs for
the brilliance of water, the bliss of tea,
or even prays to fluent gods
for life splashing and abundant to the brim—
and receives. Prayer answered?
No. How could it know
its way is in the emptying?

Awakened in the Word

"We awaken in Christ's body as Christ awakens our
bodies."

—Symeon the New Theologian

A few sank in prayer. One paced a silent anger.
Another wept. All lost in dark's skull.
No one spoke except in a cry up to him

like a hand beseeching, a longing.
His face was ashen, the flame of each miracle
at which we had warmed ourselves—

water to wine, walking on the sea,
artesian springs of quenching love—
having burned down to this. *I am the Way,*

he said, but surely he did not mean
this guttering air, these
tatters of light upon the cross,

shroud of our own agony
and our sorrow
like a curtain rent.

In his eyes' last light, we knew
his flesh, his death now ours.
Be born again, he said.

This knowing—
is it womb or grave?

To Believe

Many years ago, in a corner of our small backyard, we planted a dogwood tree. We chose dogwood because, in addition to its size and lovely spring blossoming, the tree is native to our part of North America. The dominant theme in our rather haphazardly cultivated yard is native. Since its planting, the dogwood has been joined by other natives: redbud, spicebush, Christmas fern, wild yam, jack-in-the-pulpit, wild ginger, wild columbine, spiderwort—all forest inhabitants. Prairie species and plants adaptable to both full and partial sunlight include switchgrass, lead plant, purple coneflower, Culver's root, meadow rue, hazelnut. About a third of our front yard is black-eyed Susans. Periodically, we plant and lose for one reason or another various natives. In brief, our little yard is a miniature representation of two of Ohio's historically native habitats.

One of the beauties of native trees, flowers, and grasses is that they need little maintenance and are adapted to a region's precipitation patterns. But once in a while, a drought stresses our trees and flowers. That's what happened some years back when our dogwood was about five years old. A drought hit while we were on vacation for several weeks, and there was no one to water the dogwood. It suffered, and some limbs died. I thought we were going to lose the entire tree, but the next spring, much of it had revived. Still, I ended up amputating the dead limbs. The tree no longer has the beautiful symmetry of its youth. Nevertheless, when it blossoms in the spring and leafs out in the summer, it is still quite lovely, and I enjoy looking at it from my study windows or sitting in its dappled shade.

More than convenience and beauty encouraged me to make our yard an urban haven for native plants. The poet Wallace Stevens said, "We live in the description of a place and not in the place itself." I want my experience of the Ohio River Valley to be more than what I have read and been told. I want to live aware in this place. I want to see and smell spicebush. I want the pleasure of discovering in yet another spring Jack in his pulpit in the shadows of our yard. I want to see the profusion of spring white and the brilliance of autumn leaves on our dogwood. All of this roots me in place. It anchors me to Here and, therefore, also to Now.

"Geography," Jon Levenson wrote, "is simply a visible form of theology." I suppose a tree can be theology also, but my dogwood is more than theology. It is a visible form of belief.

An old story (Appalachian in origin, I think) tells of the dogwood's role in Christ's crucifixion. In Biblical times, the story goes, the dogwood was a large, sturdy tree. Because of its strength, dogwood was the wood of choice for Christ's cross. Seeing the tree's distress at such a use, Christ promised the tree that it would never again be big enough and strong enough to be used so. The dogwood tree we know memorializes this promise and the crucifixion with its white petal-like bracts and their rusted indentations (from the nails), its crown-of-thorns flowers in the center of the bracts, and its blood-red berries (and, some add, its blood-red leaves in the autumn).

A lovely story, I think. Who knows its origin? Perhaps it came from the fertile, perceptive imagination of a devout believer contemplating the blossoming tree around Easter time. Whatever its origin, it most certainly isn't true, if for no other reason than the fact that the dogwood has never been native to the Holy Land.

But I don't care. The story has its hold on my heart anyway.

I have never been to Israel, and I doubt that I ever will visit there. I must confess that the whole Jesus story comes from a time and place so distant and a natural environment so different from mine that it seems remote and incredible. How can that story of self-denial, submission to God, and love leading to death in a distant place and time hold any immediacy and relevance for me?

Lord, I believe; help my unbelief (Mark 9:24).

And he does.

The tree answers my need, speaks to my condition. The story of the dogwood's role in the crucifixion may not be true, but nevertheless, every time I look out my study window and see our dogwood, especially in the spring, I remember the story. The tree's native immediacy reminds me of Divine Love incarnated and suffering. What I love, the Beloved, becomes more real, blossoms in my awareness here and now.

to believe

is to hold
the Beloved
in my heart
not head
(where I clench
desire
or wish
for certainty)
possible
because the heart
knows
belief
was born of love
and can embrace
how my backyard
dogwood's
four white bract petals
and nail rust
might tell
the story
of death and love
in a place
I've never seen

*The words *believe* and *beloved* share the same origin in
the Proto-Indo-European root word *to love*.

The Word

has come to be in our sentence:
    to be the name of prayer
    to be, to do
    to be who receives
    to be the *and* joining hands,
    to be among between within:
declarative imperative interrogative.

Advent

Grief like a cross
she will bear to her own dying—
she pauses under its gravity
before turning the corner
where she will see his tomb
and now wonders
at this sudden intimation
of something about to be born.

Meditation at Dawn

From this crystal silence
comes
my next moment,
my next breath,
my next prayer,
like the flesh of a lily shoot stirring
into its light,
like Christ come out in his promise,
greeting the women in the deathless morning.

The Substance and the Evidence

Watching the leaves at dawn
flutter and shimmer into day,
hearing their small voices,
I know the wind.

Take, Taste

We watch the horizon. He must be there;
he will arise resplendent through the brooding
morning clouds, we pray.
                Or we fumble
for the garden key, the promise
of the gentle whisper of cosmos,
of conversant ferns at dusk.

But here, take and taste—
the bite of berries dark as blood,
the coarse grain of the moment's bread,
the silvery lightness of living water.

Sea Change

John 3:8

The waves
are something
the wind
is saying
to the water.

On Quantum Theology

Three, they say, but One.
Father, Spirit, Son.
Wave or particle, this Light
still fills my eyes.

Second Wind

The first breath, *a priori*, became
that One we think sounded the deep, one
like a voice—the waves being something said to the water.
Then there was a falling out and eons of the same,
again and again,
until we hardly heard it, hardly felt it,
until the iterations became pillars holding a temple roof,
until we lost the breath of life,
until there was only the sound of still water,
Which is nothing.

And then new breath.
Now Wind is always—
like prairie wind.
Wind beats a branch against the dark;
you can hear the light seeping through.
Wind dances down in little dust devils,
awkward name for the raising up of earth.
It scrapes a door on a settling sill;
the door will always open.
Regardless,
it wears a film of dust from rock and us,
sings through wires and grass
(such a hymn)
and sets the aspen quaking in the moon
(delirium of light).

And, too, it curls itself up, tumbling through passes
where birds muscle their wings against its thrust.
For what, after all,
is smooth sailing that takes you nowhere?

Wind comes to the man in his bed,
defeated but listening, worn away but lifted
suddenly as if he were prayer,
and Wind sustains him.
Wind comes to the lonely woman at her window,
she who lets Wind in at her breasts,
she who feels like an immaculate mother.

And to you, breathed into being out of eternity:
feel how Second Wind fits itself to your bones.

III

fragrant bread of love

I Am Because We Are

Pebbles in a bag
rub, chafe, rasp, buff.
Good morning. Here
we are. Together again.

Warm Stone in Moonlight

Jade carved to translucence.
An ancient scholar walking
a willow-combed stream,
on the opposite bank a maiden
brushing her hair; one
oblivious, the other smiling;
the trees weeping palely
across the stone. All
these a green world.
Yet in the faces, subtle
sign of the incisive hand,
a little quaver.

Precious Seed

Framed in the open window of the rusting red door,
she's pretty as a picture; the seed of light
shines so in her brown face.
Too young to pick, old enough to be a burden,
she waits in a pickup at field's edge,
waits for another August dusk.
In the hot and hazy Ohio air, her mother and father
are bent in the field's middle distance,
vague question marks.
She watches, murmurs a child's tuneless song,
not knowing yet the songless days before her,
not knowing how she will be about her father's business.

The sun lays its dusty smolder across the field,
and a darkening veil falls over the eastern sky
under which her parents now return, faces drawn,
bearing the heavy sheaves of their days.
Her voice flutters about them in the parched light.
Was she ever a song carried in their hearts?
I imagine her mother at some past day's
hot and brittle end waiting
while her man—harrowed and harvested himself—hovers
over her, sparrow frail, embracing her with dusty wings.
No annunciation here, his finishing grunt the only Magnificat
for more fruit to be bruised at our table.

A Winter Evening

after "Winter Evening" by Georges Trakl

Snow flies from the dark against my apartment windows,
and as the first flakes melt on the warm emptiness,
a phone rings next door or down the hall—
I'm not sure where—but somewhere
    perhaps
a table is set for many,
waiting for one,
a home well provided for guests.

I imagine wandering the darkened alleys
of this floor, faces blooming gracefully
like peonies from behind elevator doors.
I step quickly aside when a latch clicks
as if pain at last is to be released.
In a sudden radiant opening,
I glimpse through a door
bread and wine glowing on a table.

Hymn

We sang, "I come to the garden alone
while the dew is still on the roses,"
but there were three of us
in the old Chevy, warm together,
rattling through the cold night toward
Grandpa,
not knowing if we would
find him home or nowhere
but determined to keep our own in the fold.
The voices I heard were ours,
not the Son of God disclosed.
Now you are all gone these many years,
but walking in my garden alone,
I hear us again
and wonder about the difference.

Grace Before Breakfast

waking from the soliloquy of dream to prayer

first light seeking my corners and crevices
               the Love that finds us
that light
               forgiving the shadows
and hence dogwood white
               rising once again
cardinal house finch song sparrow
               new songs on the wings of morning
ripples across the face of the pond
               the wind whispering to water.
somewhere near a church bell
               another answering from the valley
sky
               a silver-veined chalice
in the kitchen
               fragrant bread of love

and the day opening opening.

Sunday Morning Whiteout

All night, falling snow, a trackless silence,
and now dawn light snow-filled until
all ways across the field have failed, but still
at the table, soft voices warm as hands.

IV

new light kindled from old

About Us, Shadow Light

Shadow, you are never alone
and should not think so.

Even in the dark ice of a January night,
snowlight holds you in the field

among the grass stalks and boulders,
you born of light

and whatever rises to receive it.
And you, Light, do not be proud.

Borne through filaments of enigma,
to boulder and grass,

only in such incarnation can we know you.
Before that, who are you?

Dark essence waiting,
presence to be transposed.

Shadow Light,
featured icons of our prayers,

I hold you
in one hand.

Spirit

Spicebush, Redbud, now Dogwood—
new light kindled from old,
I bow
into your flame.

Shapes the Sunlight Takes

At God's splendid word, light
burst upon the shore as wave, then brilliant beads,

became a spin, strangeness,
charm, and then, familiar us:

a goldfinch hanging from a thistle
and bluestem billowing in the prairie morning,

a turtle feeding on a fungus
flowering from deep in a log,

a glisten, a bubble—
a spring from under moss

blue dusting the sky seen
through a tear in the forest canopy,

a man chopping wood,
the chips flying about him like sparks,

the hum and beat of blood in my ears
and the buzz in the honeycomb.

Even the full moon, though the darkening trees,
the moths beneath, an occasional glitter:

each of these sufficient, a breathing brilliance,
but all, the gold inseparable from the ring.

Transfiguration

At first a deathly still.
I think, the world is giving itself
over to fall, that bleak metaphor
of loss, of our mortality, and
the coming cold night.

ii

Beech, ash, maple
send off their leaves
in silent cadences.
Twists and turns,
a lazy downward drift,
a bobbing on waves of heat,
stem-first pirouette,
straight plummet,
a graceful helix,
a floating on the current
of the hollow's slope.

Each falls as if it knows
at last
how to yield itself to air.

iii

Oak leaves clinging to their branches
become the wind,
murmuring an ecstasy of runes,
bronze mysteries, poems
at the end of the world.

iv

Now
colors once smothered by green
have risen:
saffron, carmine, copper,
sienna, umber, purple. Not
death's shades but the stirring
of life's recollected hues.

v

A tulip tree leaf
comes into a different inspiration.
Flung upward a moment
against its own earthward calling,
it soars high above leaf litter
toward the sunny veil of the canopy.
Wind shifts, grabs it back,
but not before it's found clear sky
and glows a moment against blue,
then transfigured by light it has worn,
still wears,
brings its gold to earth.

Eucharist of Silence and Light

Sometimes I forget myself,
not absent-minded so much as present
at the altar of the hills

at dusk
when last light transfigures, crimson all over,
sweet as wine,

and silence,
bread of heaven, falls
on the tongue,

and there is nothing
but this.

Vespers

I love the solemnity
of evening trees—
how they bow into their last shadows.

Witnessing

Sitting at a small fire, I've seen
a pair of yellow eyes spark up
at the tangled brush rim of dark.

Light's not light until it's fleshed:

fireflies in the grass, a mushroom
flaring in the detritus of an oak, a swamp
log half sunk, burning
in wisps. Even a corpse left
gives off its foxfire; the old husk
flames out, swirls and spills into the night,
a coal long seething
slowly burst among the ashes.

I've seen the darkness breathed upon.

So, the shining of the world reveals itself.

Yes,

the light has slipped from dusk,
leaving night's dark robe,
but look, a rosary of stars.

The Faithful Stars

Blue sky. Moonlight. The same.
Dust in the eyes.
Only in the dark silence of prayer,
Abraham's stars.

Under a New Moon

I have come now to that time I have long heard of—
like a country I might someday live in—
but could not imagine,
and so I can hardly believe I have arrived.

It's different here than I thought.
From this horizon, I can see distances—
not the long, light-steeped days of my youth,
lived and scarcely glimpsed,
but deep, star-sculpted night distances.

Dark.
But only as tonight's new moon is dark.
Silent.
Still, not the voiceless provinces of dread.

There is an inherence, the promise of the carver's block,
and I begin to listen for all
that can be said without words.

A heedless passing through the light brought me here.
Now I will trust the night, will make my way,
feeling, perhaps, more than seeing the path,
farther and farther
into the opening reaches.

V

a blessing has arrived,
and I am left to rest lightly here

Crossings

I watch the sky, that metaphor:
soon dark will crest and break across my yard as dawn,
the first of the day's crossings I will see,
    the first change borne.

It's metaphor that makes the world—
Milhaud's saxes angling blues and cakewalking trumpets,
Emily with a bee and a clover and a reverie,
    Yahweh with starlight and breath.

From here to there or there,
over each horizon a line is traversed in some way,
and in the crossing, something is born anew,
    each a poem.

In noon's heat,
I've watched the harbor wind spill
in wave and rise again as bell toll,
    spill and rise as toll.

A pasture fence is true
until wind opens geometry, and the sheep amble
over, transubstantiated, eccentric snowflakes
    nuzzling deep clover.

I've known a hand to lift
a stone from its gravelly sleep: glass shatters,
a face appears, gasps on the fresh blue air,
  and words become a starburst.

There now: the sun's risen.
A window's thrown open on green fields waiting.
Perhaps a roan is about to glimmer over the ridge
  from the bright space beyond the hill.

In a corner of the pond,
reeds explode into red-winged blackbirds scolding,
and in the breeze, a spray of light rises, blowing
  to the Queen Anne's lace.

These are gifts, all gifts,
the way a kiss is a gift at any time,
lips that become my breath and blood,
  gifts of otherness.

For each day's gifts
stretch and fling out into dance, for all waters
become heady wine, all bread become flesh; give
  thanks for these daily poems.

Pearl of Great Price

I found this moment
just now
and have already sold tomorrow
to buy it.

Savor

for Fred Middendorf

Taste and see.
Let these words, the paradox
of delicious air, become lambent wine,

serve the alchemy of regard—
say, the mushroom's meaty prayer
rising from the forest floor—

say, silvery lightness of living water
or the sweet eucharist of a berry.
Of course, you'll know always

ambivalence of hunger and desire—
salt of longing lingering on the tongue,
coarse grain of the moment's bread—

but always, too, the need to savor.
Even that bitter sight, the beautiful cloud of crows
across winter's dusk, the look of silence

they leave behind.

This

So this is emptiness.
So this is the awakened heart.
Wood thrush song, then a moment's cease.
Wind now and again in the pines.

Attention

Call it to the moment.
Draw all eyes to its blossom
and gather it like rosebuds.
Pay this debt to Presence
before Time
itself flags.

Telling the Beads of Silence

I

When the quiet comes, something.
The wind dies a moment, and in that lull,
a story speaks that hasn't yet been told;
in a line's caesura, another poem;
between the evanescent temple bells
speaking in tongues, a prayer.
But what's at the center of the ripple
the stone's plunge makes?
What's under the slip of water over rock?
And what is this rising in my heart's nave
where I kneel
amidst shuffling feet and rustle of genuflection?

II

When you hear

not the stone's plunge
but what's at the center of its ripple,

what's under the slip of water over rock,

what's left after
the winnowing wind,

what's between the temple bells'
speaking in tongues,

what's in your heart's nave
amid the shuffling feet—

that is,

when you hear
how that seed of silence
is as Light—

that is,
any moment, now.

Compost

The nip and zip of radishes,
the peels of bananas in their brown study of fade, and
oranges ringing their brighter change, peas
split to earthy broth,
the small potatoes
of our daily consuming,
even bread of family communions ended
broken from wholeness—
              slice, flake, molecule—
the piecemeal detritus of our hungering.

Behold!
The squash blossom
arising
from muck and mold.

A Wren at Twilight as the Gate

In my yard, a Carolina wren, its crystal singing
mandala and tingsha bell in one.

In such intricate clarity of breath,
the eventful light draws down

to a silver thread thinning,
fading from the blue dusk,

taking me with it,
and way opens,

leaving now
night, an empty mirror.

After Reading Merwin's
"For the Anniversary of My Death"

After all those years of passing through that ritual day
and my body slyly observant
(what those heart-in-the-mouth
and legs-gone-numb moments are about?)
and that holy day dawns (closes?), what will it be like?

Oh, I like to imagine Death
tripping at the threshold, stumbling
into a tangled skein of tubes,
an IV bag flopping on its shoulder,
a veritable Buster Keaton of end times.
Off I'll go, giggling, moonwalking from the light
center stage into the dark wings.

Or maybe I'll go quietly, embraced
(reluctant darling) by death's painful imperatives,
perhaps glancing back longingly.
Or maybe it will be in a lightless fright
like a hand suddenly on my shoulder.

Somehow, this Gordian knot
of friend, son, husband, father
will be slashed, undone.
I'll shed the strange garments of who I am,
slough selves like a snake.

I'll leave behind a silence,
my irrefutable absence sucking from my witnesses
fading images of my eyes, my voice;
the memory of how I touched my wife;
how I held my liquor, my minutes, my disappointments;

until finally someone says, "Franchot Ballinger,"
one last time, and another day, someone will pause,
puzzled, and wonder what she's forgotten,
something she meant to bring along.

Is that it: Death's last sting?

But leaving what? Being what?

What? No white stone with a new name?

What about the last scene of 2001, the star child
floating in its placental bubble to earth again?
Can't I sail into some stranger's womb
like thistle fluff into a distant field?
How would I be known? Would I know myself?

No? No?

Ah, well. All this death talk.
I believe.

Cut the air with a knife.

When the vase breaks,
the air inside and out flows together
like those long-separated lovers, river and sea.

For three days rain closed me in,
and I watched myself, a shadow in the windows,
but it's lifted now, and a Carolina wren—
bird resurrected from deep, deep winter,
bird of belief in new light now light—
calls from far in the red cedars,
last of their kind in the forest.
What sounded like whichistheday whichistheday
becomes thisdaynow thisdaynow.

The Way

Leaf litter covers the yard,
late winter shroud and
mantle of coming resurrection—
unquiet earth.

All and in All: A Natural History

Here or there, you'll find the same measure.

Crack open a stone,
God is there, a flinty spark
leaping lightly to a flame in the Dance.

Crumble the shards of a hollow, rotting log,
and on your fingertips is the moist, warm breath of the Spirit
whispering through the wreath of being.

And see the early spring seed-bound white
of the dogwood where Christ—his last gasps
the first fragrant winds of love—flowers again.

Opus Dei

Vigils

> Awake from soliloquies of dream,
> no longer the lost communicant,
> I feel the brooding, silent
> dark, how it has held me
> and at my first prayer becomes
> early light, the promise
> of more from that first—
> of day's coming feast,
> this, my morning's Eucharist.

Lauds

> With morning's wings I lift
> on thermals of bright grace,
> and in this light mend night's rift
> with arabesques of praise.

Terce

> Like pollen rising
> from sunlit pines,
> I too
> would bear the light.

Sext

A soaring redtail's fixed against
the blue, its cry like nails driven in.
In hoc signo vinces—
not in battle's gore
but in the mercy of this hour.
Oh, Windhover,
slayer slain
wings whispering
of death becoming life,
hold my dead weight aloft
in those murmurings of grace.

None

An hour of death
day's heat gathers,
shroud of weariness,
water light reflecting
off leaves day,
suddenly mute,
sorrow silence.

Vespers

How the swifts dip and swoop.
Again and again, they cross.
Spirit beads I tell on ribbons of praise
before the coming sleep.

Compline

There comes a waiting quiet
when I shall sleep a space,
a death in dreams, but grace
makes dark the light,
waiting
for the matter of my heart.

Resting Lightly Here

Something snaps outside,
and I startle up from sleep, or near sleep,
having been only at its weedy fringes
half-expecting something
in the dark that's seeped into my tent
over and around my mummy bag.

Other sounds—the *tingsha* bell of tree frogs,
the katydid's strident gossip, a whip-poor-will's
redundancy—fall
back into the blur of silence.

There are brown bears in these woods—
seldom seen—but still,
couldn't one come upon me suddenly,
something raging from the shadows?

My caught breath is heavy as the dead-still, leaf-mold air.
Night has collapsed into itself, and I am held in fraught dark,
held, as if possessed. Something is here,
filling the air about me, grave and belly dark,
bear medicine, even if no bear.

The Mayans say, at night the sun hides inside the jaguar.
I imagine how it flares like a match struck, flashing
in the dark before them the living, killing face of God. Why not,
then, this rustle and twig snap, the breathing dark,
        as the still, small voice?

I let go, and I'm released in a moment's artesian clarity.
Here at the forest edge, I reach out in the night,
open like a moonflower, like a prayer.

Through some unbidden step, my measure has been taken,
a blessing has arrived,
and I am left to rest lightly here.

The Estuary: September

once again
a hush
comes over the land

always this
from the drift
things are then pass
in the braided stream
this then that

chittering cicadas
the gourd swelling and the walnut
thistle down in the winnowing wind
swallows folding another day under their wings
neighbors' voices soft in the cooling nights

the sky shape-changing
above the forests gone mute
in a brown study
what the summer storms have meant
and what the close days have left

these grains of time
each
in its own time
once
this then that

now once again
released
into the still autumn waters

Cycle

Thirst of a clear blue sky,
longing of water for down.
Which is the way of prayer?
Heaven and earth are one.

VI

"Where can I find the man who has forgotten words?"

—Chuang Tzu

Ode to Writer's Block

O you bluenose nixing every erect sentence;
some mornings something sticks like peanut butter
on my palate, and I can't tongue it loose.

No bubbles rise as from bottom-stirring turtles
or from the decay of thought,
or from some diver deep in the coral of inspiration.
No diver either.
Clouds pass before my eyes,
a confusion of inexplicable weather.
The sun rises, it snows, then
the puzzling calligraphy of winter trees.
There are words everywhere.
Even the waves are something
the wind is saying to the water.

O,
to be a word and fly
over the walls of your empty city,
and to become!

But you arrive like the DEA,
throw me up against the wall,
hang a sign outside: "Closed by order of. . . ."
Words scatter. Who knows where?
Out open windows, to cellar corners,
fugitives clutching
their nickel bags of thought.

Isn't this silence
a sickness unto death?
Is it true, then—
no word, no thing?
Can no thing matter?
Surely, every thing matters.
In certainty, I must
make some thing matter.

I will take you as the midnight hour
when even breath is steeped in meaning.

Wordless, I will know you as the tongue
that was mine before I was born.
Maybe you will be the gate to God,
the one of the voiceless night,
that one in the silence between the stars,
the wordless Word abiding in emptiness.

O,
take then my breath
as offering, this aphasia
as atonement.

Acknowledgments

Grateful acknowledgment is made to the editors of the following print and online publications in which many of these poems in an earlier version or their present form first appeared.

Aji
    "Ode to Writer's Block," Spring 2015 #2
Ancient Paths
    "Take, Taste," March 3, 2005
Birmingham Arts Journal
    "This," April 2018
Blue Unicorn
    "Crossings," June 2006;
    "Cain killed Abel," February 2011
    "About Us, Shadow Light," 38.2
    "Passion Painting with No Goldfinches,"
        October 2015
    "That Moment," October 2017
Candelabrum
    "Love and All the Green," July 2001
    "Resting Lightly Here," October 2001
    "Warm Stone in Moonlight," July 2002
Cincinnati Poetry Review
    "A Winter Evening," Spring 1988

Comstock Literary Review
    "In the Dark Belly of Assumption," Spring/
        Summer 2001
For a Better World
    "Floating in This Dark," June 2004
    "Precious Seed," April 2008
    "Sanctified Church"; "Snow Furies," April 2010
Friends Journal
    "The Substance and the Evidence," September
        2006
    "Sunday Morning Whiteout," November 2017
Poetry Life and Times
    "Adam, Where Are You?" May 9, 2015
    "The Love of One Woman," October 8, 2015
Presence
    "Telling the Beads of Silence," March 2017
Quaker Life
    "Awakened in the Word," October 2016
    "The Faithful Stars," April 2017
    "Open Worship," October 2017
    "Released," January 2018
    "Opus Dei," April 2018
    "Grace Before Breakfast," October 2018
Quantum Poetry
    "Under a New Moon," January 31, 2012
Red Fez
    "Keeping the Distance," December 13, 2013
RFD
    "A Wren at Twilight," Spring 2003
School of the Spirit Snapshots
    "Transfiguration," October 24, 2018
    "To Believe," March 14, 2019

The Lyric
>"Cold Spell," Winter 2010
>"When I Remember Thee upon My Bed,"
>>Winter 2017

The Penwood Review
>"Shapes the Sunlight Takes," Fall 2005
>"Advent," Spring 2012
>"On the Hope-Thin Highwire," Spring 2014

Windhover
>"Meditation at Dawn," January 2006
>"This Cup," January 2006

Franchot's family would like to thank everyone at Fernwood Press for making this book a reality. We would especially like to thank Eric Muhr for his dedication to seeing this book published and for patiently answering our many questions as we navigated this new-to-us process.

Thank you to Dan Kasztelan, who set this book in motion when he suggested Franchot send his manuscript to Fernwood Press. Many thanks to Heather Shumaker for her insights and advice. Lastly, deep gratitude to Kevin Griffith for generously sharing his time, energy, and the wisdom of his experience.

Title Index

First Line Index

V

W

www.ingramcontent.com/pod-product-compliance
Lightning Source LLC
Chambersburg PA
CBHW010857090426
42737CB00020B/3403